introduction

JUST DO THE NEXT RIGHT THING

No matter how old you are or what stage of life you're in, you will always have decisions to make. Some of those decisions will have noticeably life-changing consequences or life-shaping outcomes, but many of them will seem tiny and rote. The daily choices you make aren't always monumental, but they are always there. In fact, it's estimated that adults make over thirty-five thousand decisions every single day. One by one, those decisions are quietly, steadily making your life.

As each day rolls into the next, you're led through one life transition after another—potentially one fog after another—always looking for the clearings, always watching for hope, always listening for clues that you're headed in the right direction. Even the most grounded and professional among us can suffer from decision fatigue given the right set of circumstances.

When I'm in a season of transition, waiting, or general fogginess, the best and most approachable advice I've ever received is to simply do the next right thing. Authors Anne Lamott and Brennan Manning both have their own version of this advice, as do

Martin Luther King Jr., Theodore Roosevelt, and Mother Teresa. For decades it's become a common catchphrase spoken by coaches in locker rooms and leaders in boardrooms, and it is a lifeline for those in the recovery community. And while he didn't say this exact phrase (that we know of, anyway), Jesus's entire life was marked by living day by day, listening to and caring for those in his path, and simply doing the next right thing in love. The phrase has been such a fixed point for me that I started a podcast called *The Next Right Thing* where I dedicate each short, weekly episode to a thoughtful story, a little prayer, and a simple next right step for listeners.

We want to do the right thing but sometimes don't trust ourselves to know what the right thing is. We worry we'll choose the good but miss the best. We're concerned that maybe we are too late or too early. We fear we'll miss out, miss the boat, or miss the point. We overanalyze options, potentials, and possibilities. We consider what our family thinks, what our friends think, and what everyone else thinks we should do in a particular situation. Meanwhile, we're suspicious of our own desire, fearing that what we want may not be what God wants. If only we could make life decisions with more confidence and clarity.

Before getting too caught up in the pressure to do the right thing, consider this: the beauty of doing the next right thing isn't necessarily found in the word *right* but in the word *next*. To do the right thing may sound easy in general, but in the midst of a foggy transition, it can be hard to know what that is. But to do the *next* right thing is more friendly, accessible, and hopefully possible.

If you're struggling through a transition, carrying a heavy bag filled with unmade decisions, or worried about choosing the right thing for your life whether you're fifteen, twenty-five, or fifty, this journal is here to serve as a fixed point for you through every decision-making season of your life.

◐ ◐ ◐

After the release of *The Next Right Thing* book, I heard from readers and friends who said they loved the prayers and practices at the end of every chapter but wished they had a place to record their progress, capture seasonal reflections, and explore on a more personal level the impact their decisions were having on their everyday lives. Not only did I nod my head in agreement, but these requests served as an invitation for me to dive even deeper into my own practice of weekly, monthly, and seasonal reflection.

Intentional list-making is a key part of my own decision-making process, and for years I had several different journals for capturing these different kinds of lists and reflections. But if there's one thing I know for sure, it's that when we're suffering from chronic hesitation or decision fatigue, the last thing we need is a stack of half-used blank journals to choose from. We need prompts, guidance, and a dependable place to make a list. Essentially, this is the tool I've always wished I had, a guided journal for decision-making all in one place.

WE DO NOT LEARN FROM AN EXPERIENCE . . . WE LEARN FROM REFLECTING ON AN EXPERIENCE.

—JOHN DEWEY, *HOW WE THINK*

why use this journal

This journal is not a daily planner for your to-do lists, and neither is it a goal-setting workbook for you to record your progress. Instead, it's a companion for life-giving decision-making, and it is rooted in reflection.

One common mistake we make when we have the desire to make good decisions is that we try to peer into the future to discover what it might hold, what the outcomes we want to achieve are, and what roadblocks we wish to avoid. This is a natural tendency and is often what we're encouraged to do. The only problem is the future hasn't happened yet, so how can it possibly teach us? Instead of looking ahead and guessing about outcomes, let's look back and gather information. The best indicator of life-giving decisions for the future is paying attention to choices we've made in the past.

If you are a person who loves that magical week between Christmas and the new year, this journal will be your new best friend. For many of us, that week is an in-between collection of days where a lot isn't expected of us in terms of our schedule, so we may have a little extra time to pay attention to our soul. We look back over the year, think over what was good and not so good, and consider how we want to move into the year to come. What a beautiful practice.

Unfortunately, while that week of reflection is helpful, it may be the only time we intentionally reflect all year.

Essentially, in this journal we'll take the posture of that final week of the year and spread it out over the course of twelve months. And by the way, this can be *any* twelve months. You may pick up this journal in January and work through it until December. But if you start it in April or September, that will work just as well. Think in terms of ninety-day blocks rather than particular months of the year, and you'll be just fine.

If reflection doesn't come naturally to you, you're still in the right place. Maybe you have the desire to be more intentional with the decisions you make and the way you spend your days but have no idea where to start. We'll do this together, and we'll take it slow.

This journal exists to help you discern your next right thing by paying attention to your last right thing and your right-now life. Ideally, this resource will be a kind companion for you over the course of a year, guiding you through monthly and seasonal questions, reflections, and intentions. The goal is not to work your way through it for the sake of finishing; the goal is to walk your way through it for the sake of listening to your life.

Maybe you want to make better decisions. But what if you could also learn to make them in a better way? No more late-night pro/con lists, frantic calls to friends, or last-minute doubting and second-guessing about a decision you've already made. With these intentional reflections, prompts, and simple lists, you'll begin to recognize personal patterns and preferences while gaining valuable perspective about what is life-giving and life-draining in this season of your life.

If you picked this book up because you have a decision to make and want help making it, hear this: one of the simplest ways to make more informed decisions in your life is to reflect on decisions you've already made. Our choices define our lives, not just the ones we're carrying right now about our future, but also the ones we've made in our past. Wouldn't we do well to bring them to mind and see what they have to teach us?

When I go through life without reflection for too long, I feel like I'm only half-human. I forget who I am, what I most long for, and where I'm headed. I walk around with a list of to-dos scribbled on the back of a crumpled receipt in the bottom of my purse and a low-grade panic in the pit of my soul. Have you been there?

The practice of looking back and paying attention serves as an anchor for the soul in a fast-moving world. Instead of waiting for the world to stop so we can catch up, we slow ourselves, look around, and name what we see.

When I'm paying attention to the public road I'm walking and my private world within, I tend to be more patient, more kind, more willing to give myself and others grace. I am able to notice what God is up to within me and around me. We are humans, not robots. We have the capacity to not only make choices but to learn from choices we've made. So let's get started.

how to use this journal

If you've already read *The Next Right Thing* book, then the following may likely be familiar to you. Either way, here is a brief explanation for the rhythms, prompts, and lists you will find in the pages that follow.

A RHYTHM OF REFLECTION MADE SIMPLE

Many have the desire to be more aware of life as they live it, to capture memories and reflect on past decisions to inform future ones. But without guidance, it can be difficult to know where to start and what to look for. The format for this guided journal will keep you on track with weekly, monthly, and seasonal reflection practices.

SEASONAL

We are created to live rhythmically in the rhythms of creation. Seven days repeated in a sequence of four weeks place us in the rhythm of the twenty-eight-day phase of the moon circling the earth. . . . We are immersed in rhythms. But we are also composed of rhythms. Physiologically we live out rhythms of pulse and breath. Our hearts beat steadily, circulating our blood through our bodies in impulses of

> sixty or eighty or a hundred times a minute. . . . We are embedded in time, but time is also embedded in us.*

If God had made the world straight up and down, we would have no seasons or change, just the sun shining straight at the equator all year round. Instead, he chose to tilt our world on its axis, making a way for strawberries, red leaves, quiet snow, raging hurricanes, spring showers, and sunflowers standing high in salute.

The way the world tilts, turns, and rotates on a predictable rhythm we can measure and count on year after year is equal parts comforting and mysterious. God built a rhythm into creation around us, and it is mirrored within us: in birth, life, death, hellos, goodbyes, joys, and sorrows. We carry this rhythmic pattern with each inhale and exhale that sustain us.

The tilt made a way for long light as well as long darkness. The tilt made a way for change. The earth moves, sometimes giving and sometimes taking, then spinning around and giving something or taking something back again. As we reflect on our lives, let's take our cues from the built-in rhythm of the world. All good stories have both darkness and light, and so it goes with us.

When we stand at the end of one season and the starting edge of the next, it's tempting to race right into the future without considering the season we've just moved through. But that costs us something, and we may not realize it until we approach that same season a year later. Reflecting on a seasonal basis is a gift to your future self and can prevent overcommitment to things that don't much matter.

With the following pages divided into four repeated sections, you're invited to look at your life according to the seasons. Just

* Eugene Peterson, *Christ Plays in Ten Thousand Places* (Grand Rapids: Eerdmans, 2008), 68.

as the seasons cultivate different growth patterns in nature, this rhythm is seen in us as well. Themes of waiting and listening in the dark tend to rise to the surface during the wintertime, while themes of growth and new life emerge in spring.

MONTHLY AND WEEKLY

While big-picture reflection is important during each season, it will be made easier if we are also paying attention at the end of every month. Throughout each month will be questions for reflection, simple prayers and practices, quotes for remembering, and even a monthly quote page for you to place a quote that's currently meaningful for you. Once per month, you're invited to record the books you've read or are reading as well as the art you're enjoying (podcasts, music, movies, shows). You may also keep a weekly record of what the days hold in your "These Are the Days" lists, explained below.

A LIST OF LISTS

Lists are simply a tool we use so we don't forget things. We make grocery lists so we don't forget bananas and to-do lists so we don't forget to take the dog to the vet or sign the permission slip. But lists can be good for other things too; namely, things going on in us beneath the surface. Our lives are always telling us a story. But is the story true? How can we know for sure? The first step is to pay attention, and an easy way to do that is to make a list.

- **These Are the Days (weekly):** Each month includes a two-page spread of four blank lists with this heading. You may want to use one list per week to simply record a list of what your current days look like, bullet-point style. It's not meant to be a narrative description but more of a big-picture glance. What are the things these days hold?

- **A List of Gratitude (monthly):** You need not sit down and write down what you're thankful for all at once. If it comes out that way, lovely. But you may return to this list over the course of the month and write down things as they come, a way of paying attention as you go along. What are you grateful for this month?
- **A List of Questions (monthly):** The decisions we are required to make in our lives begin first as questions. *Which schooling choice is best for our kids? How can I care for aging parents? How will I pay the bills when I don't have a job? When is the best time to sell the house?* Every day we carry questions, and we may not realize how many. This monthly list is a place to record the questions you're carrying all in one place so you can have a birds-eye view of decisions you may need to make each month.
- **A Life Energy List (monthly):** This is one tool to help you pay attention to your actual life so that you can discern what your next right thing might be, allowing past decisions to inform future ones. This may be the most important list of all because it's one that helps you to intentionally discern your yes and your no before the time comes to make the decision in the first place. This list is meant to be preemptive, not reactive. It won't eliminate your need to decide things when decisions come your way, but it could serve as a helpful filter for future decisions.

  To fill out your monthly Life Energy List, simply ask yourself two questions: In the past month, what was life-draining? What was life-giving? It may help to do this by categories such as work, schedule, family activities, business partnerships, travel, deadlines, relationships, volunteer commitments, and/or daily routines. There's no wrong way to do this as long as you are truly honest about the things that bring life and the things that drain life. It can be tempting to judge ourselves when making these lists, thinking certain activities or commitments should bring life when in fact they do not. The more honest you are, the more informed your decisions will be.

The goal for this list is not to eliminate everything on the life-draining list. That's not realistic or even wise. We will always have things we have to do no matter how we feel about them. But we will also have things in our life we say yes and no to based on habit, fear, or expectation. This list can help us know what they are. You may discover your life-draining list is actually filled with things you can opt out of. On the other hand, you may have something listed on your life-giving list you would like to incorporate more often. These are things to pay attention to.

Another way of asking these two key questions (life-draining and life-giving) could be this: Over the last month, what pushed me from God (life-draining) and what drew me to God (life-giving)? Remember, there are no wrong answers. What is life-giving or life-draining for you may be different from me. And what is life-giving to you now may be draining for you six months from now.

- **A List of Arrows (monthly):** When we have questions, it's natural to want answers. Instead what we usually get are arrows: not a full answer, but maybe one next right thing. When we have decisions to make, sometimes the answer comes all at once but more often the answers emerge in a slow unfolding. God often gives us a faint vision of things before they ever come to be. It's not a full form, more of a shadow, unfocused and unclear. These arrows don't come with sure things or solid instruction, but they do come with hope. As you consider the questions recorded at the beginning of the month, here is where you can keep track of the arrows as they emerge during the month.

- **A Happy List (monthly):** This is a list to record what you've read, watched, listened to, and made this month, from books to music to podcasts, lectures, or conversations. Did you make a budget or a scarf? Did you read a fantastic article? Did you write a song or a poem? What a happy list of things to remember!
- **A Look-Ahead List (quarterly):** Look ahead at the next three months and consider six primary areas of activity. Do you have any **travel** plans scheduled over the next three months? What **deadlines** will come across your desk? What does **family** life hold? What **celebrations** or anniversaries need to be considered? Will you be **hosting** guests? What will be happening in your **community** this season? We do not make decisions in an empty room. We need to consider how our lives will be impacted in each season, so it's important to remind ourselves what each season will hold.
- **What I Learned (quarterly):** Oprah calls it one of her most embarrassing moments, when film critic Gene Siskel asked her on live television, "What do you know for sure?" and she didn't have an answer. After that, she did a lot of thinking about the things she knows for sure, and this is often a question she asks others. That story inspired me to consider what I knew for sure, but I found that to be a complicated list to keep. Instead, I

realized I would rather explore the step that comes *right before* what I know for sure—that's a list of what I'm learning.

This is a friendly, fluid list to keep as you pay attention to your life. It allows room for you to hold experiences in your hands, walk around with them, ask questions, and sometimes set them down and consider if it's time to leave them behind. This list can be comprised of anything you're learning about anything, whether it's silly, simple, or sacred. These lists will serve as a quarterly reminder that you aren't just *doing things* but are *becoming someone*. Who are you becoming? What are you learning along the way?

These eight lists will repeat throughout this journal, guiding you through twelve months of reflection and intentional list-making to help you discern your next right thing. You can always refer back to these descriptions to remind yourself of the intended purpose of each list, but of course you're free to make this journal your own and use the lists in whatever way makes sense for you. Most of all, I hope you will fill these pages with honest words about your right-now life so you can discern your next right thing in love.

○ ○ ○

GOOD DECISIONS REQUIRE CREATIVITY,
AND CREATIVITY REQUIRES SPACE.
STILLNESS IS TO MY SOUL AS DECLUTTERING
IS TO MY HOME. BECOMING A SOUL MINIMALIST
DOES NOT MEAN THAT YOU SHOULD
HOLD ON TO NOTHING BUT THAT
NOTHING SHOULD HAVE A HOLD ON YOU.

○ ○ ○

SEASON

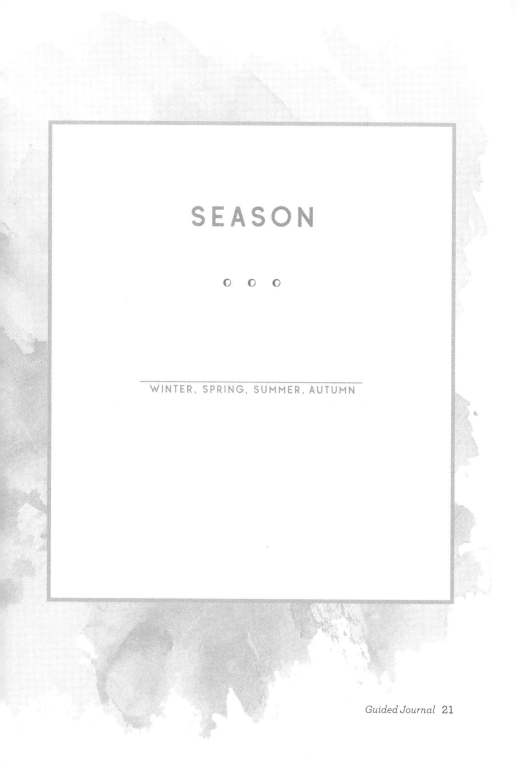

WINTER, SPRING, SUMMER, AUTUMN

A PRACTICE: NOTICE THE SILENCE

Silence may be more accessible than you think. Begin to notice the naturally silent spaces in your days—the first light of morning, your office space when you arrive early, the walk to the mailbox, your apartment before your roommate gets home from work, the drive to the grocery store. Rather than filling these times with sound or holding on to the soul clutter by rehearsing past conversations or future possibilities, decide instead to let yourself be quiet inside the silence. Write down what you hear.

THE QUIET YOU FIND IN STILLNESS CAN SERVE AS A COLANDER, *helping you discern what you need to hold on to and what can fall gently away. What is one thing cluttering your mind that you can let go of today?*

A LOOK-AHEAD LIST FOR ________________ (SEASON)

TRAVEL

DEADLINES

FAMILY

CELEBRATIONS

GUESTS AND HOSTING

COMMUNITY

REFLECTIONS FOR ______________________ (SEASON)

I WANT...

I NEED...

I HOPE . . .

A PRAYER

We confess we live distracted lives, and our insides often shake with constant activity.

We have grown accustomed to ignoring our low-grade anxiety, thinking that it's just a normal part of an active life.

This might be typical, and it might be common. But let it not be normal.

Instead of trying to figure out how to calm the chaos and hustle around us, we rejoice with confidence that we don't have to figure our way back to the light and easy way of Jesus, because you have already made your way to us.

We have your Spirit living within us, which means there's hope for us after all.

You invite us into each moment to simply do the next right thing in love.

A QUOTE FOR THE MONTH

MONTH

THESE ARE THE DAYS . . . ___/___/___

THESE ARE THE DAYS . . . ___/___/___

THESE ARE THE DAYS . . .

___/___/___

THESE ARE THE DAYS . . .

___/___/___

A GRATITUDE LIST

I will give thanks to the LORD with all my heart; I will tell of all your wonders. —*Psalm 9:1*

A LIST OF QUESTIONS

Every decision begins as a question.
What questions are you carrying into this month?

-
-
-
-
-
-
-
-

A LIFE ENERGY LIST

WHAT WAS LIFE-DRAINING THIS MONTH?

WHAT WAS LIFE-GIVING THIS MONTH?

Often the clues to our next decision remain within us, unheard and undiscovered. When we take the time to follow those clues, we might find we are holding on to some things we no longer need.

A PRACTICE

The way we make decisions is equally as important as the decisions we make. Choice is one of the primary avenues of our spiritual formation. What are some things you're thinking about pursuing, starting, quitting, making, finishing, or embracing?

*If you don't see the clear path, the endgame, or the five-year plan, take heart. Be excessively gentle with yourself. Get still. Stop talking. Pause the constant questioning of everyone else's opinion. Now hold these things, whatever they are, one by one in your mind. Pay attention to your body and your soul—*Does it rise, or does it fall? *This can serve as one indicator that you're moving in the right direction.*

A LIST OF ARROWS

When we have questions, it's natural to want answers. Instead what we usually get are arrows: not a full answer, but maybe one next right thing. As you consider the questions you've been carrying this month, are any arrows emerging?

›

›

›

›

›

›

›

A HAPPY LIST

READ

WATCHED

LISTENED

MADE

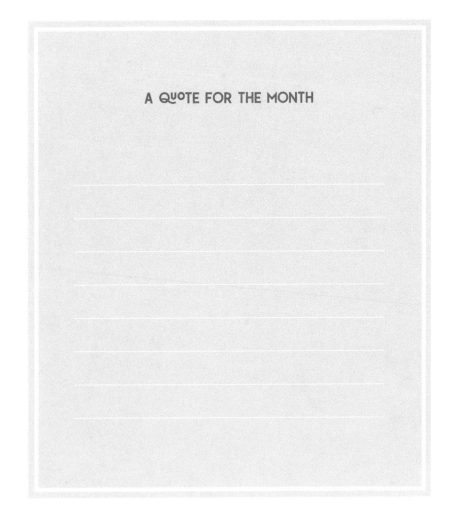

A QUOTE FOR THE MONTH

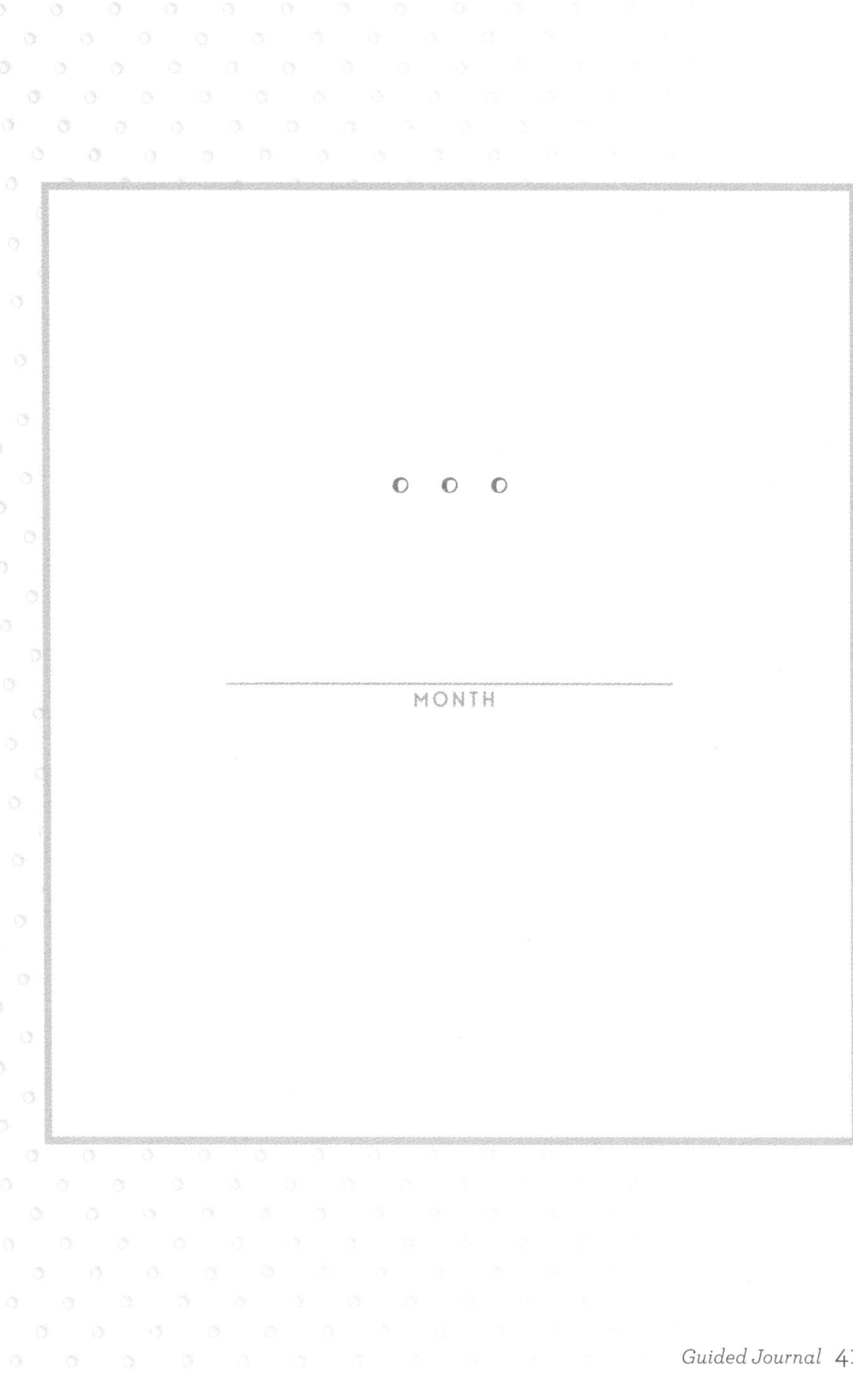

MONTH

THESE ARE THE DAYS . . .

__/__/__

THESE ARE THE DAYS . . .

__/__/__

THESE ARE THE DAYS . . .

__/__/__

THESE ARE THE DAYS . . .

__/__/__

A GRATITUDE LIST

Moments of gratitude for the strangers who have walked with me fill my life constantly. There is always a return gift waiting in my heart. —Macrina Wiederkehr, Seasons of Your Heart

A LIST OF QUESTIONS

Every decision begins as a question.
What questions are you carrying into this month?

-
-
-
-
-
-
-
-

A LIFE ENERGY LIST

WHAT WAS LIFE-DRAINING THIS MONTH?

WHAT WAS LIFE-GIVING THIS MONTH?

You are loved with an everlasting love and underneath are the everlasting arms. —Elisabeth Elliot

A PRACTICE

One cause of hesitation in decision-making is because things remain unnamed within us. Below are questions that could help your unnamed realities rise to the surface today.

Is there a hurt you haven't quite let go?

A regret that's been following you for so long you think it's normal?

An excitement you haven't given yourself permission to explore?

A dream that might be hanging out in the wings, kicking at rocks, or standing on tiptoe?

Did one of your children just start kindergarten or go off to college?

Did you or your spouse start a new job?

Is there someone in your family with a recent diagnosis?

Is a friend celebrating a success you wish was yours?

An important part of the decision-making process is naming the unnamed things. If one of these questions helps you to name a reality, write it down. If not, consider what else might need naming in your right-now life.

There is power in naming the unnamed things. This is an important part of our decision-making practice and key to taking our next right step in love. Remember today is a plot point. See it honestly for what it is, but don't confuse the moment for the whole story.

A LIST OF ARROWS

When we have questions, it's natural to want answers. Instead what we usually get are arrows: not a full answer, but maybe one next right thing. As you consider the questions you've been carrying this month, are any arrows emerging?

›

›

›

›

›

›

›

A HAPPY LIST

READ

WATCHED

LISTENED

MADE

A QUOTE FOR THE MONTH

MONTH

THESE ARE THE DAYS . . .

___/___/___

THESE ARE THE DAYS . . .

___/___/___

THESE ARE THE DAYS . . .

___/___/___

THESE ARE THE DAYS . . .

___/___/___

A GRATITUDE LIST

O give thanks to the Lord, for He is good; for His loving-kindness is everlasting. —1 Chronicles 16:34

A LIST OF QUESTIONS

Every decision begins as a question.
What questions are you carrying into this month?

-
-
-
-
-
-
-
-

A LIFE ENERGY LIST

WHAT WAS LIFE-DRAINING THIS MONTH?

WHAT WAS LIFE-GIVING THIS MONTH?

God will not shame you into better behavior. He will not trick you. He will not tease you. He will not laugh at you. He will not terrorize you. He does not pull rugs out from under you. He does not drop the other shoe. He does not pull fast ones. He will not roll his eyes, throw up his hands, or turn his back on you.

A PRACTICE

When you close your eyes and imagine God, what is the first thing you see? Are there colors, shapes, or outlines? Do you see a face, a hand, the curve of a shoulder? What emotion rises up in you, if any? What is the look on his face? What about yours?

What we believe about God informs every aspect of our lives, including our decisions.

A LIST OF ARROWS

When we have questions, it's natural to want answers. Instead what we usually get are arrows: not a full answer, but maybe one next right thing. As you consider the questions you've been carrying this month, are any arrows emerging?

›

›

›

›

›

›

›

A HAPPY LIST

READ

WATCHED

LISTENED

MADE

WHAT I LEARNED THIS SEASON

Don't be afraid to be a beginner. Be relentlessly kind to yourself. What if this is your next right thing?

NEVER BELIEVE ANYTHING BAD ABOUT GOD.

—DALLAS WILLARD

o o o

SOMETIMES THE CIRCUMSTANCES AT HAND

FORCE US TO BE BRAVER THAN WE

ACTUALLY ARE, AND SO WE KNOCK

ON DOORS AND ASK FOR ASSISTANCE.

SOMETIMES NOT HAVING ANY IDEA

WHERE WE'RE GOING WORKS OUT BETTER

THAN WE COULD POSSIBLY HAVE IMAGINED.

—ANN PATCHETT, *WHAT NOW?*

o o o

SEASON

WINTER, SPRING, SUMMER, AUTUMN

A PRACTICE

Consider a decision you are facing this season that feels particularly difficult to resolve. Write down the decision below. (Hint: If you can't put it into a sentence, then you may not have a decision to make yet.) Then describe why this decision feels particularly difficult for you (the timing, the people involved, the finances required, and so on).

IN THIS DECISION, ARE YOU BEING LED BY LOVE OR PUSHED BY FEAR?

What is the worst thing that could happen? What is the best thing that could happen?

A LOOK-AHEAD LIST FOR ______________________ (SEASON)

TRAVEL

DEADLINES

FAMILY

CELEBRATIONS

GUESTS AND HOSTING

COMMUNITY

REFLECTIONS FOR ______________________ (SEASON)

I WANT...

I NEED...

I HOPE...

A PRAYER

Unbound by time or place or gravity, you go ahead of us into an unknown future.

When you declare your love for us, we refuse to squirm away.

When you offer good gifts, we receive them with gratitude.

When you delay the answers, we wait with hope.

We resist the urge to sprint ahead in hurry or lag behind in fear. Let us keep company with you at a walking pace, moving forward together one step at a time.

Help us to know the difference between being pushed by fear and led by love.

A QUOTE FOR THE MONTH

MONTH

THESE ARE THE DAYS . . .

__/__/__

THESE ARE THE DAYS . . .

__/__/__

THESE ARE THE DAYS . . .

__/__/__

THESE ARE THE DAYS . . .

__/__/__

A GRATITUDE LIST

Rejoice always; pray without ceasing; in everything give thanks; for this is God's will for you in Christ Jesus.
—1 Thessalonians 5:16–18

A LIST OF QUESTIONS

Every decision begins as a question.
What questions are you carrying into this month?

-
-
-
-
-
-
-
-

A LIFE ENERGY LIST

WHAT WAS LIFE-DRAINING THIS MONTH?

WHAT WAS LIFE-GIVING THIS MONTH?

Is the life that you're living the same life that wants to be lived in you? Before you tell your life what you intend to do with it, listen for what it intends to do with you. —Parker J. Palmer, Let Your Life Speak

A PRACTICE

For the next twenty-four hours, practice pausing when someone asks your opinion on simple things, such as where to eat lunch, which outfit looks better, or what the order of events should be at the meeting. Pausing is important no matter if your personality is hesitant or assertive. If you're hesitant, the pause could serve as a good reminder: *what you want matters.* If you're traditionally more assertive and say what you want quickly, the pause could help you discern what you want *more*. This is a mini version of our decision-making practice: create space, name the unnamed things, and do the next right thing.

Knowing what we want is not the same as getting what we want, and certainly not the same as demanding what we want. When I honestly admit what I most long for in the presence of Jesus, I can more quickly accept when it doesn't work out. I can talk to him about it, admit my heartbreak, and receive what he has to give in place of it.

A LIST OF ARROWS

When we have questions, it's natural to want answers. Instead, what we usually get are arrows: not a full answer, but maybe one next right thing. As you consider the questions you've been carrying this month, are any arrows emerging?

›

›

›

›

›

›

›

A HAPPY LIST

READ

WATCHED

LISTENED

MADE

A QUOTE FOR THE MONTH

MONTH

THESE ARE THE DAYS . . . ___/___/___

THESE ARE THE DAYS . . . ___/___/___

THESE ARE THE DAYS . . .

___/___/___

THESE ARE THE DAYS . . .

___/___/___

A GRATITUDE LIST

Eucharisteo—thanksgiving—always precedes the miracle.

—Ann Voskamp, One Thousand Gifts

A LIST OF QUESTIONS

Every decision begins as a question.
What questions are you carrying into this month?

-
-
-
-
-
-
-
-

A LIFE ENERGY LIST

WHAT WAS LIFE-DRAINING THIS MONTH?

WHAT WAS LIFE-GIVING THIS MONTH?

If you feel more like a robot with a to-do list in your hand than an artist with wonder in your eyes, stop. Close your eyes, open one hand in your lap and put the other on your heart, and ask yourself, What am I longing for in this moment? What is life-giving?

A PRACTICE

Take a quiet moment and ask yourself these questions: Is now the time for me to quit something? Am I working hard toward something only to realize it isn't quite right anymore? Has my heart changed on an issue but my mind has yet to get the memo?

There is a time for everything, and a season for every activity under the heavens: a time to be born and a time to die, a time to plant and a time to uproot, a time to kill and a time to heal, a time to tear down and a time to build, a time to weep and a time to laugh, a time to mourn and a time to dance. —Ecclesiastes 3:1–4 NIV

A LIST OF ARROWS

When we have questions, it's natural to want answers. Instead what we usually get are arrows: not a full answer, but maybe one next right thing. As you consider the questions you've been carrying this month, are any arrows emerging?

›

›

›

›

›

›

›

A HAPPY LIST

READ

WATCHED

LISTENED

MADE

A QUOTE FOR THE MONTH

MONTH

THESE ARE THE DAYS . . .

___/___/___

THESE ARE THE DAYS . . .

___/___/___

THESE ARE THE DAYS . . .

__/__/__

THESE ARE THE DAYS . . .

__/__/__

A GRATITUDE LIST

Oh give thanks to the LORD, for He is good; for His loving-kindness is everlasting. —Psalm 106:1

A LIST OF QUESTIONS

Every decision begins as a question.
What questions are you carrying into this month?

A LIFE ENERGY LIST

WHAT WAS LIFE-DRAINING THIS MONTH?

WHAT WAS LIFE-GIVING THIS MONTH?

Resist the urge to scold yourself when you feel scattered. Remember, no one has ever been shamed into freedom.

A PRACTICE

Consider one thing that feels overwhelming this month, causing you to flit into the future and make imaginary plans or fret over potential outcomes. Write what that is on the lines below. For example, you might write: "I'm concerned about a conversation I have to have with my supervisor."

Then turn your worry into a question and add the word *today* on the end. For example, "Do I have to have a conversation with my supervisor today?" If the answer is yes, ask yourself, *What is the next right thing I can do now as it relates to this concern?* If the answer is no, you have some time to consider your next right thing. Either way, you can't do everything today, but you can do one thing at a time.

O God, gather me now to be with you as you are with me.

—Ted Loder, Guerillas of Grace

A LIST OF ARROWS

When we have questions, it's natural to want answers. Instead what we usually get are arrows: not a full answer, but maybe one next right thing. As you consider the questions you've been carrying this month, are any arrows emerging?

›

›

›

›

›

›

›

A HAPPY LIST

READ

WATCHED

LISTENED

MADE

WHAT I LEARNED THIS SEASON

God meets us where we are, not where we pretend to be.

—*Dr. Larry Crabb,* Real Church

MAY YOU LEARN TO SEE YOURSELF WITH THE SAME DELIGHT, PRIDE, AND EXPECTATION WITH WHICH GOD SEES YOU IN EVERY MOMENT.

—JOHN O'DONOHUE,
TO BLESS THE SPACE BETWEEN US

○ ○ ○

THE STEPS OF A MAN ARE ESTABLISHED BY THE LORD,

AND HE DELIGHTS IN HIS WAY.

WHEN HE FALLS, HE WILL NOT BE HURLED HEADLONG,

BECAUSE THE LORD IS THE ONE WHO HOLDS HIS HAND.

I HAVE BEEN YOUNG AND NOW I AM OLD,

YET I HAVE NOT SEEN THE RIGHTEOUS FORSAKEN

OR HIS DESCENDANTS BEGGING BREAD.

ALL DAY LONG HE IS GRACIOUS AND LENDS,

AND HIS DESCENDANTS ARE A BLESSING.

—PSALM 37:23–26

○ ○ ○

SEASON

○ ○ ○

WINTER, SPRING, SUMMER, AUTUMN

A PRACTICE

If you've been searching for clarity that isn't coming, it could be time to let go of your timeline. Some work has to grow slow:

- the idea that takes years to form
- the ministry that needs darkness and time to bury its roots down deep into you
- the book that only wants to drip out of you, one slow word at a time
- the business that requires an unrushed foundation

Write down decisions that are taking a long time to sort through.

INSTEAD OF FOCUSING ON WHAT YOU NEED TO DO, IS THERE ANYTHING YOU NEED TO *UNDO*? *What might God be inviting you to let go? What do you* want *to do? If that one's hard to answer, why?*

A LOOK-AHEAD LIST FOR ______________________ (SEASON)

TRAVEL

DEADLINES

FAMILY

CELEBRATIONS

GUESTS AND HOSTING

COMMUNITY

REFLECTIONS FOR ________________ (SEASON)

I WANT...

I NEED...

I HOPE . . .

A PRAYER

The Prayer of St. Francis

Lord, make me an instrument of your peace:
where there is hatred, let me sow love;
where there is injury, pardon;
where there is doubt, faith;
where there is despair, hope;
where there is darkness, light;
and where there is sadness, joy.
O Divine Master, grant that I may not so much seek to be consoled as to console,
to be understood as to understand,
to be loved as to love.
For it is in giving that we receive,
it is in pardoning that we are pardoned,
and it is in dying that we are born to eternal life.
*Amen.**

* As quoted in Shane Claiborne and Jonathan Wilson-Hartgrove, *Common Prayer Pocket Edition: A Liturgy for Ordinary Radicals* (repr. Grand Rapids: Zondervan, 2012).

A QUOTE FOR THE MONTH

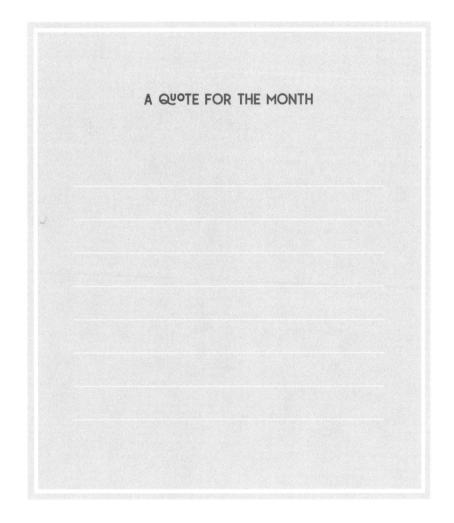

MONTH

THESE ARE THE DAYS . . .

___/___/___

THESE ARE THE DAYS . . .

___/___/___

THESE ARE THE DAYS . . .

___/___/___

THESE ARE THE DAYS . . .

___/___/___

A GRATITUDE LIST

Every good thing given and every perfect gift is from above, coming down from the Father of lights, with whom there is no variation or shifting shadow. —James 1:17

A LIST OF QUESTIONS

Every decision begins as a question.
What questions are you carrying into this month?

-
-
-
-
-
-
-
-

A LIFE ENERGY LIST

WHAT WAS LIFE-DRAINING THIS MONTH?

WHAT WAS LIFE-GIVING THIS MONTH?

It's a slow work, building a life. But the future always comes.

A PRACTICE

Make an appointment with your email inbox or, if it makes more sense, with your work desk, your bookshelf, your calendar, or your social accounts. Who are you learning from and listening to? Pay attention without judgment. Resist the urge to draw a conclusion at first. Just let yourself notice and be curious about what story these writers, teachers, marketers, and mentors are teaching you. Discern if now is the time for them. It might be helpful to consider:

- What is coming up in your life in the next ninety days?
- What can you reasonably prioritize in that amount of time?
- What practical help do you need for the journey?

Reveal to us the story our inboxes, mailboxes, bookshelves, and journals are trying to tell us. Help us pay attention to what we pay attention to.

A LIST OF ARROWS

When we have questions, it's natural to want answers. Instead what we usually get are arrows: not a full answer, but maybe one next right thing. As you consider the questions you've been carrying this month, are any arrows emerging?

›

›

›

›

›

›

›

A HAPPY LIST

READ

WATCHED

LISTENED

MADE

A QUOTE FOR THE MONTH

MONTH

THESE ARE THE DAYS . . .

__/__/__

THESE ARE THE DAYS . . .

__/__/__

THESE ARE THE DAYS . . .

___/___/___

THESE ARE THE DAYS . . .

___/___/___

A GRATITUDE LIST

Let the peace of Christ rule in your hearts, to which indeed you were called in one body; and be thankful. —Colossians 3:15

A LIST OF QUESTIONS

Every decision begins as a question.
What questions are you carrying into this month?

-
-
-
-
-
-
-
-

A LIFE ENERGY LIST

WHAT WAS LIFE-DRAINING THIS MONTH?

WHAT WAS LIFE-GIVING THIS MONTH?

God is less interested in where we end up than he is in who we are becoming.

A PRACTICE

If you have a decision you feel unable to resolve, it may be time to find some co-listeners. Think about the people in your life who have some (or all) of these qualities, people who:

- ask thoughtful questions
- listen for the answers
- don't belittle you or say things that make you feel dumb
- don't take themselves too seriously
- take you just seriously enough

Finally, make a short list of people (maybe four to eight) you would consider asking to be part of a co-listening group. Consider people from your church, college friends, neighbors, family members, couples you admire, or longtime family friends. If you can't think of anyone, that's okay. Now you know what to look for.

If you're standing at the crossroad of transition and you aren't sure which way to go, as you seek people in your life who can stand beside you, and as you are becoming a person who stands beside others, take heart—the Lord is always with you and within you, beside you and before you. He is not impatient, he is not angry, and he is not overwhelmed by you. He is not frustrated, fed up, or afraid. He is filled with compassion toward you and his banner over you is love.

A LIST OF ARROWS

When we have questions, it's natural to want answers. Instead what we usually get are arrows: not a full answer, but maybe one next right thing. As you consider the questions you've been carrying this month, are any arrows emerging?

›

›

›

›

›

›

›

A HAPPY LIST

READ

WATCHED

LISTENED

MADE

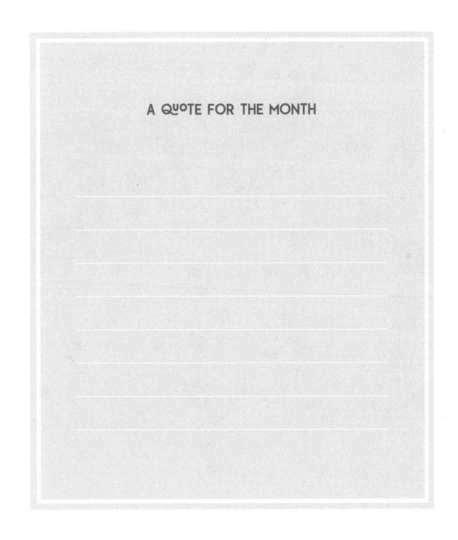

A QUOTE FOR THE MONTH

MONTH

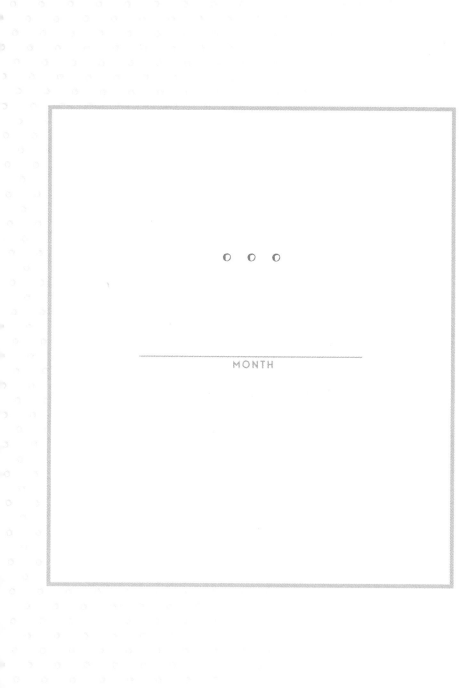

THESE ARE THE DAYS . . .

___/___/___

THESE ARE THE DAYS . . .

___/___/___

THESE ARE THE DAYS . . .

___/___/___

THESE ARE THE DAYS . . .

___/___/___

A GRATITUDE LIST

Be anxious for nothing, but in everything by prayer and supplication with thanksgiving let your requests be made known to God. —*Philippians 4:6*

A LIST OF QUESTIONS

Every decision begins as a question.
What questions are you carrying into this month?

-
-
-
-
-
-
-
-

A LIFE ENERGY LIST

WHAT WAS LIFE-DRAINING THIS MONTH?

WHAT WAS LIFE-GIVING THIS MONTH?

May we continue to cultivate a strong no in our lives so that we can say more life-giving yeses.

A PRACTICE

Always remember that, in the kingdom of God, all things are being made new, including our poorly chosen yeses. Even so, past decisions can help inform future ones.

Reflect on a time in your life when you said yes to something only to realize later it was perhaps not a wise yes. What was the situation surrounding that yes? Did anyone encourage or discourage you in that decision? What was the outcome?

Now think of a time when you said a brave no to what many might consider a great opportunity. What was the situation surrounding that no? Did anyone encourage or discourage you in that decision? What was the outcome?

When it comes to making decisions, combatting decision fatigue, and learning to trust our own heart in the presence of God, we have to be careful who we allow in. Don't give your critic words.

A LIST OF ARROWS

When we have questions, it's natural to want answers. Instead what we usually get are arrows: not a full answer, but maybe one next right thing. As you consider the questions you've been carrying this month, are any arrows emerging?

›

›

›

›

›

›

›

A HAPPY LIST

READ

WATCHED

LISTENED

MADE

WHAT I LEARNED THIS SEASON

The daily guarantee that, if we will only begin the journey and stay the road—listening to the voice of God and responding to it with all our gifts and goodness—we will find that God stands waiting to sustain us, and support us, and fulfill us at every turn. God is calling us lovingly always, if we will only stop the noise within us long enough to hear. —Joan Chittister, The Monastery of the Heart

JUST BECAUSE THINGS CHANGE DOESN'T MEAN YOU CHOSE WRONG IN THE FIRST PLACE. JUST BECAUSE YOU'RE GOOD AT SOMETHING DOESN'T MEAN YOU HAVE TO DO IT FOREVER.

○ ○ ○

IF YOUR LIFE IS A CONSTANT BLUR OF ACTIVITY, FOCUS, AND OBLIGATION, YOU ARE LIKELY TO MISS CRITICAL BREAKTHROUGHS BECAUSE YOU WON'T HAVE THE BENEFIT OF PACING AND NEGATIVE SPACE. WHAT'S NOT THERE WILL IMPACT YOUR LIFE AS MUCH OR MORE THAN WHAT IS.

—TODD HENRY, *THE ACCIDENTAL CREATIVE*

○ ○ ○

SEASON

○ ○ ○

WINTER, SPRING, SUMMER, AUTUMN

A PRACTICE

Next time you stand in the garden center, the classroom, the office, the paint store, the library, the sanctuary, the grocery store, or the ice cream shop, accept that there may not be a perfect choice, a right choice, or an ideal. Instead, pick what you like, then see how it grows. Write down your experience.

MAKE A LIST OF WHEN YOU HAVE FELT MOST LIKE YOURSELF.

Where were you? Who were you with? What were you doing?

A LOOK-AHEAD LIST FOR ________________ (SEASON)

TRAVEL

DEADLINES

FAMILY

CELEBRATIONS

GUESTS AND HOSTING

COMMUNITY

REFLECTIONS FOR ______________________ (SEASON)

I WANT . . .

I NEED . . .

I HOPE...

A PRAYER

As we stand at new beginnings and grieve those long goodbyes, teach us what it means to hold on to what we need for the journey and gently let the rest go.

Father, you bring new mercies every morning and give us the grace to start over as many times as we might need.

Keep pace with us as we learn to keep pace with you.

Thank you for not rolling your eyes when we find ourselves here again.

Give us the courage to pick what we like and the patience to see how it grows.

A QUOTE FOR THE MONTH

MONTH

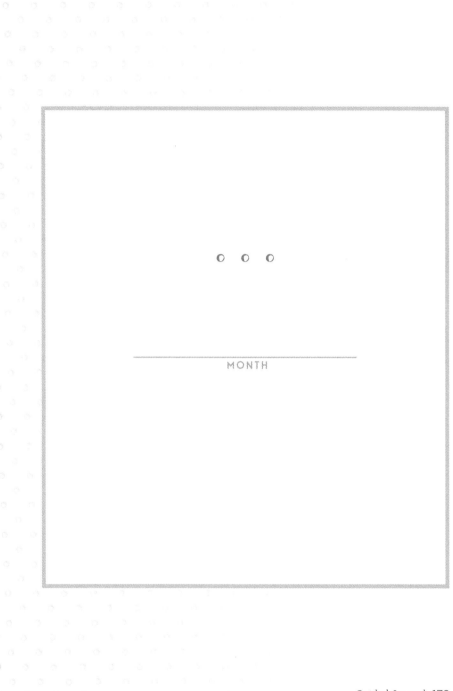

THESE ARE THE DAYS . . .

__/__/__

THESE ARE THE DAYS . . .

__/__/__

THESE ARE THE DAYS . . .

___/___/___

THESE ARE THE DAYS . . .

___/___/___

A GRATITUDE LIST

Devote yourselves to prayer, keeping alert in it with an attitude of thanksgiving. —Colossians 4:2

A LIST OF QUESTIONS

Every decision begins as a question.
What questions are you carrying into this month?

•

•

•

•

•

•

•

•

A LIFE ENERGY LIST

WHAT WAS LIFE-DRAINING THIS MONTH?

WHAT WAS LIFE-GIVING THIS MONTH?

According to Jesus, everything we think we know about winning has to do with losing. Everything we think we know about gaining has to do with letting go. —Deidra Riggs, One

A PRACTICE

Anything can be a spiritual discipline if we remember the presence of God with us in it. God is with you in every ordinary moment, no matter how small. Make a list of activities or practices that draw you closer to God. It may be some traditional things like praying or reading Scripture, but you may also include some quirky just-for-you things.

Practicing a spiritual discipline is not about trying to earn something, prove something, or win. Practicing a spiritual discipline is more about receiving power to live in the kingdom.

A LIST OF ARROWS

When we have questions, it's natural to want answers. Instead what we usually get are arrows: not a full answer, but maybe one next right thing. As you consider the questions you've been carrying this month, are any arrows emerging?

›

›

›

›

›

›

›

A HAPPY LIST

READ

WATCHED

LISTENED

MADE

A QUOTE FOR THE MONTH

MONTH

THESE ARE THE DAYS . . .

___/___/___

THESE ARE THE DAYS . . .

___/___/___

THESE ARE THE DAYS . . .

__/__/__

THESE ARE THE DAYS . . .

__/__/__

A GRATITUDE LIST

Counting your blessings is a powerful spiritual exercise. Pay attention to the details of your life. Look for the hidden things.
—James Bryan Smith, The Good and Beautiful God

A LIST OF QUESTIONS

Every decision begins as a question.
What questions are you carrying into this month?

-
-
-
-
-
-
-
-

A LIFE ENERGY LIST

WHAT WAS LIFE-DRAINING THIS MONTH?

WHAT WAS LIFE-GIVING THIS MONTH?

Making a living is nothing if you're not also making a life.

A PRACTICE

Author and teacher Jan Johnson emphasizes the importance of listening to God in our everyday moments, often asking *What does it look like for you to walk with God for the next ten minutes?*

True ministry is not something we do but is the overflow of an abiding life with God.

A LIST OF ARROWS

When we have questions, it's natural to want answers. Instead what we usually get are arrows: not a full answer, but maybe one next right thing. As you consider the questions you've been carrying this month, are any arrows emerging?

›

›

›

›

›

›

›

A HAPPY LIST

READ

WATCHED

LISTENED

MADE

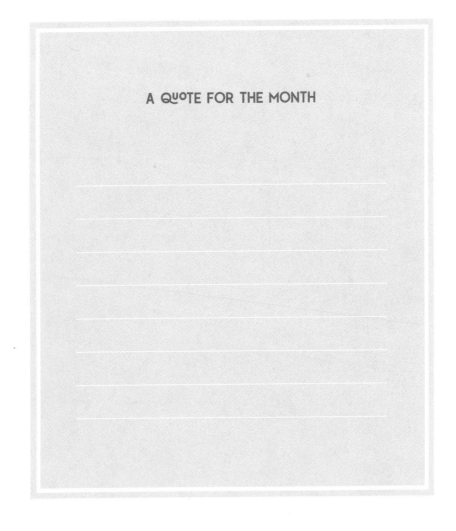

A QUOTE FOR THE MONTH

MONTH

THESE ARE THE DAYS . . .

__/__/__

THESE ARE THE DAYS . . .

__/__/__

THESE ARE THE DAYS . . .

__/__/__

THESE ARE THE DAYS . . .

__/__/__

A GRATITUDE LIST

You will be enriched in every way so that you can be generous on every occasion, and through us your generosity will result in thanksgiving to God. —2 Corinthians 9:11 NIV

A LIST OF QUESTIONS

Every decision begins as a question.
What questions are you carrying into this month?

A LIFE ENERGY LIST

WHAT WAS LIFE-DRAINING THIS MONTH?

WHAT WAS LIFE-GIVING THIS MONTH?

Let's embrace the courage to choose what's best and the faith to come back when we choose what isn't.

A PRACTICE

When is the last time you were surprised by God?

As we make plans, fill out lists, and do the things that need doing, may we remember to remain open to surprise. Instead of insisting on clear plans, may we be willing to settle in and take the next right step even though it may lead someplace we didn't quite pack for.

A LIST OF ARROWS

When we have questions, it's natural to want answers. Instead what we usually get are arrows: not a full answer, but maybe one next right thing. As you consider the questions you've been carrying this month, are any arrows emerging?

›

›

›

›

›

›

›

A HAPPY LIST

READ

WATCHED

LISTENED

MADE

WHAT I LEARNED THIS SEASON

It's not a black-and-white world, which means decisions aren't always as simple as either right or wrong. It doesn't always matter which road you choose. What matters is God is with you.

JUST DO THE
NEXT RIGHT THING
IN LOVE.

what I learned this year

books I read this year:

what worked for me in the last twelve months:

what did not work for me in the last twelve months:

resources

Here are some resources for decision-making guidance from specific chapters and episodes of *The Next Right Thing* book and podcast.

WHAT'S YOUR DECISION-MAKING STYLE?

- Episode 74: "What's Your Decision-Making Style?"
- Quiz: When it comes to making decisions, do you tend to lead with your head, your heart, or your intuition? Take the quiz at emilypfreeman.com/quiz.

HOW TO MAKE THE MOST OF THE LISTS IN THIS JOURNAL

THE LIFE ENERGY LIST

- Episode 3 and Chapter 9: "Make the Most Important List"

QUESTIONS AND ARROWS

- Episode 16: "Walk Slow and Carry Questions"
- Episode 24: "Look for Arrows (Not Answers)"
- Chapter 5: "Look for Arrows"

WHAT I LEARNED LISTS

- Episode 4: "Record What You Learn"
- Episode 61: "Look Behind You—How Reflection Can Help You Make Better Decisions"
- Episode 84: "A Beginner's Guide to Self-Reflection"

DOES GOD CARE ABOUT ME AND THE DECISIONS I HAVE TO MAKE?

- Chapter 4: "Picture God"
- Episode 23: "Release Your Agenda"
- Episode 65: "Take Off Your Crown"
- Episode 111: "Never Believe Anything Bad about God"

HOW CAN I KNOW WHAT I REALLY WANT?

- Episode 14 and Chapter 8: "Know What You Want *and* Know What You Want More"
- Episode 25 and Chapter 19: "Come Home to Yourself"
- Episode 32 and Chapter 15: "Stop Collecting Gurus"
- Episode 34 and Chapter 20: "Pick What You Like"
- Episode 50: "Go Forward to Something"

HOW DO I FIND CLARITY?

- Episode 1 and Chapter 2: "Become a Soul Minimalist"
- Episode 27 and Chapter 12: "Stop Rushing Clarity"

- Episode 48: “Receive the Waiting Time”
- Episode 58: “Welcome Silence”
- Episode 70: “The Best Time to Make a Decision”
- Episode 97: “Find Ten Minutes of Clarity”

WHAT IF I KEEP SECOND-GUESSING MYSELF?

- Episode 2 and Chapter 7: “Do This before Every Hard Decision”
- Chapter 23: “Expect to Be Surprised”
- Episode 75: “Tell Yourself the Truth”

WHAT IF I MAKE THE WRONG DECISION?

- Episode 66: “Don’t Let the Ending Define the Whole Story”
- Episode 68: “If You’re Afraid of Making the Wrong Decision”
- Episode 79: “Find Relief from Regret”
- Episode 82: “Find the Beginning in the Ending”

WHAT IF I’VE CHANGED MY MIND?

- Episode 13 and Chapter 10: “Quit Something”
- Episode 29: “Remember the Real Art”

WHAT IF I DON’T KNOW WHAT I’M DOING?

- Episode 22: “Embrace Your Limits”
- Episode 31 and Chapter 6: “Be a Beginner”
- Episode 33 and Chapter 15: “Gather Co-Listeners”

HOW CAN I CREATE SPACE FOR MY SOUL TO BREATHE?

- Episode 72: "Design a Rhythm of Life"
- Episode 76: "Create a Simple Morning Routine"
- Episode 88: "Come Away for Awhile"
- Episode 90: "Start with This Simple Rhythm"
- Episode 108: "Walk at Your Own Pace"

ten questions to help you make a decision

1. What decision needs to be made? In one sentence, write it down. (If you can't write it down in a clear sentence, you won't be able to make a clear decision.)
2. For now, release what you think you *should* do. What do you *want* as it relates to this particular decision?
3. When you hold this decision before you, pay attention to your body. Does it gently rise or does it slightly fall? Do you light up or feel heavy? Do you feel hope or dread?
4. Is there something you're afraid of? If so, what? Or maybe, who?
5. What is the worst thing that could happen as a result of your decision?
6. What is the best thing that could happen?
7. If your decision requires a yes or no and you must choose right now, what would you choose?
8. If you can't make your decision now, can you write down (or make up) a deadline?
9. What else do you need to know before you can make a decision? (For example, what specific information, clarification, or feeling are you waiting for?)
10. What is one next right step you can take now toward making a final decision?

recommended reading

Hearing God: Developing a Conversational Relationship with God by Dallas Willard

A thoughtful perspective on listening to God, laying out your request and questions before him, and trusting that if God has something to say, he's going to make it clear.

Let Your Life Speak: Listening for the Voice of Vocation by Parker J. Palmer

A kind companion to remind you to pay attention to the shape of your own soul, especially if you have doubts about or decisions to make involving your vocation.

You Learn by Living: Eleven Keys for a More Fulfilling Life by Eleanor Roosevelt

Inspiration for keeping a What I Learned list: What vital principles do you now know because you've been paying attention, and how will what you've learned by living shape the rest of your life?

Essentialism: The Disciplined Pursuit of Less by Greg McKeown

A business book about getting only the right things done (as opposed to getting more done in less time). If decision fatigue has you feeling stuck, this book could bring clarity.

Don't Overthink It: Make Easier Decisions, Stop Second-Guessing, and Bring More Joy to Your Life by Anne Bogel

If overthinking and worrying are your habit, this book can help you break it. No more wasted energy on second-guessing!

The Listening Life: Embracing Attentiveness in a World of Distraction by Adam S. McHugh

One reason why making decisions is difficult is because we're busy acting, doing, fixing, and responding before truly listening. This book will teach you how to listen first.

Survival Guide for the Soul: How to Flourish Spiritually in a World That Pressures Us to Achieve by Ken Shigematsu

Stop the frantic looking around for answers and, instead, quiet the noise and distractions of cultural, societal, and professional pressure and truly connect with God.

What Now? by Ann Patchett

A short, practical guide for anyone standing at the threshold of an ending, a new beginning, or an uncertain transition.

Emily P. Freeman is the *Wall Street Journal* bestselling author of *Simply Tuesday* and *The Next Right Thing*. She earned her MA in Christian spiritual formation and leadership from Friends University, and she lives in North Carolina with her husband and their three children. Connect with her on Instagram @emilypfreeman.

Be sure to explore Emily's other resources for better decision-making practices: find *The Next Right Thing* book wherever books are sold, and *The Next Right Thing* podcast at thenextrightthingpodcast.com or on your favorite streaming service.

EMILYPFREEMAN.COM

ONE LAST THING

I AM ONE IN WHOM CHRIST DWELLS AND DELIGHTS. I LIVE IN THE STRONG AND UNSHAKABLE KINGDOM OF GOD. THE KINGDOM IS NOT IN TROUBLE AND NEITHER AM I.

—JAMES BRYAN SMITH